IT'S YOUR MONEY

WHAT EVERYBODY NEEDS TO KNOW ABOUT PERSONAL FINANCE

Howard J. Levine C.P.A.

First Edition

Van Nuys, California
ISBN: 978-1-7332595-1-4
Library of Congress Control Number: 2019908854

CONTENTS

INTRODUCTION

Without goals, and plans to reach them, you are like a ship that has set sail with no destination.

—Fitzhugh Dodson, author

A goal without a plan is just a wish.

—Antoine de Saint-Exupéry, writer and pioneering aviator

Always plan ahead. It wasn't raining when Noah built the ark.

—Richard Cushing, American prelate of the Roman Catholic Church

Your future is unpredictable. No matter how hard you try, you really don't know what is in store for you in the upcoming weeks, months and years. You almost certainly have personal goals, desires and wishes that you would like to accomplish.

Most of us plan for a job, classes we take at school, even what we are going to eat for lunch, but ignore our financial health. Don't feel alone—about 70% of Americans are in the same boat!

This book is divided into three parts covering a different stage in life. Within the parts, each chapter will give you basic, important information that you can use now. Don't be afraid or intimidated that you will encounter a lot of math or complicated concepts. Instead, you will come across ideas you may have heard but never really understood. The goal of this book is for you to not just learn these concepts but also put them into action, *now*.

Financial literacy is important for each and every one of us, something to take seriously to better shape and safeguard our futures. The sooner you start, the better it is for you.

As Alan Lakein famously said, "Failing to plan is planning to fail."

This book is designed to promote financial literacy with basic information. Prior to making any financial decisions, you should be sure to do your research and contact a qualified professional for assistance.

PART 1

THE BASICS

Studies have shown that early college years can be some of the most stressful in your life. Between school, work and family obligations, three are a lot of demands!

This section is designed to help you, a college student, relieve some of your financial stress and uncertainty. As you read each topic, go slowly and be sure to do the "action items" right away, while they are on your mind.

It is never too early to plan your financial success!

CHAPTER 1

BUDGET YOUR WAY TO FINANCIAL SECURITY

> *A budget tells us what we can't afford, but it doesn't keep us from buying it.*
>
> —William Feather, 1949

> *You are no longer a boy, and one of the first duties which a man owes to his friends and to society is to live within his income.*
>
> —Thomas Hughes, *Tom Brown at Oxford*, 1861

> *Budgeting has only one rule: Do not go over budget.*
>
> —Leslie Tayne, *Life & Debt: A Fresh Approach to Achieving Financial Wellness*, 2014

A *budget* is a plan for coordinating income and expenses. For many people, the "B-word" conjures up unpleasant images of self-denial and endless recordkeeping. As you will see, budgeting does not have to be painful. The rewards always outweigh the challenges.

Creating a Budget

Think about your sources of income. Whether you use an Excel sheet or the old-fashioned pencil-and-paper approach, the act of creating a budget is the same. You start by listing all sources of monthly income, including wages and salary, bonuses and commissions, interest, dividends and any other income. Sure, some of them will be approximations, but make an educated guess based on what you realistically think you will earn.

Think about your expenses. Identify your major expenses. Consider fixed monthly expenses, such as mortgage or rent, insurance premiums, child care and utilities. Next, consider your more flexible and intermittent expenses, like food, clothing, dental bills, gifts and car repairs. Don't just guess; it is helpful to review your checking account, debit and credit card statements to ensure you found all of your expenses. Don't be surprised if you spend more than you think; that is common!

Budget savings. When thinking about your budget, put aside something for savings. There are always unexpected bills, so having a "nest egg" is critical to your financial health.

Be complete. You are likely to find that some spending is hard to reconstruct and your records reflect only a portion of your spending—all those cash outlays for Starbucks seem to fall between the cracks! If you can't account for a large chunk of your spending, try carrying a small notebook for a few weeks to track the cash that you spend. While spending $5 a day on incidentals may seem trivial, the $150 you would have at the end the month certainly is not.

Budget Template

It is easy to create a budget using a simple Excel sheet. Or, you can use this example:

Monthly Budget

Month of ____________			
CATEGORY	Budget Amount	Actual Amount	Difference
INCOME			
Salary/Wages (after taxes and other deductions) Job 1			
Salary/Wages (after taxes and other deductions) Job 2			
Interest and Dividends			
Other Income			
INCOME SUBTOTAL			
FIXED EXPENSES			
Rent or Mortgage Payment			
Telephone/Cell Phone			
Insurance (home, auto, health, life, disability, etc.)			
Car Payment(s)			
Credit Card Payment(s)			
Student Loan Payment(s)			
Other Fixed Expenses			
FIXED EXPENSES SUBTOTAL			
FLEXIBLE EXPENSES			

Monthly Budget (continued)

Month of ____________			
CATEGORY	Budget Amount	Actual Amount	Difference
Groceries			
Transportation (gas, repairs, tolls, bus, etc.)			
Medical/Dental (not including insurance)			
Utilities (gas, electricity, etc.)			
Education			
Personal Services (laundry, toiletries, haircuts, etc.)			
Child Care			
Other Flexible Expenses			
FLEXIBLE EXPENSES SUBTOTAL			
DISCRETIONARY EXPENSES			
Savings			
Dining Out			
Clothes			
Gifts			
Entertainment/Recreation/ Movies/Events			
Vacation			

Monthly Budget (continued)

Month of ____________			
CATEGORY	Budget Amount	Actual Amount	Difference
Books/Magazines/Subscriptions (including digital)			
Charity			
Other Discretionary Expenses			
DISCRETIONARY EXPENSES SUBTOTAL			
TOTAL EXPENSES			
NET INCOME or (DEFICIT) (income less expenses)			

Monitor Your Progress

A budget is just a plan. It is important that you monitor your budget regularly. At the end of the month, record and categorize the current month's income and expenses. Then compare what you actually spent to what you budgeted and see how you did.

Rework the numbers. If, when you compare your income and expenses, you find that your spending is outpacing your income, you may need to rework the numbers. Try to squeeze a little out of several categories rather than taking a bigger chunk out of one.

Don't ignore cuts to your seemingly fixed expenses. For example, is it possible to reduce your mortgage payment by refinancing? Can you reduce your homeowners' or automobile insurance premiums by raising the deductible, changing carriers or selling a car you don't use anymore? Do you really need three streaming cable services, or would one do just fine?

Budgeting is ongoing. It could take several months (or more) before you arrive at a budget you can live with. The key is to be flexible. If you find you are spending more than planned, you may have to strengthen your resolve, or perhaps your goal was unrealistic and needs to be adjusted. On the other hand, maybe you are now able to save even more than you could have possibly imagined!

Action Items

- Use the previous example or an Excel sheet to come up with a budget for the coming month.
- Track your expenses, and at the end of the month, see how close you came to staying within your budget.
- Adjust the budget for the following month, and once again, see how well you did.
- Don't just do it once or twice; make this an ongoing part of your life.

CHAPTER 2

HOW TO PAY FOR COLLEGE

An investment in knowledge always pays the best interest.

—Benjamin Franklin

College is the reward for surviving high school.

—Judd Apatow, comedian

College is fun as long as you don't die.

—Tsugumi Ohba, manga author

It's hard to quantify the full value of an education. But U.S. Bureau of Labor Statistics (BLS) data consistently show that, in terms of dollars, education makes sense.

The more you learn, the more you earn. Median weekly earnings in 2017 for those with the highest levels of educational attainment—doctoral and professional degrees—were more than triple those with the lowest level. And the higher the level of education, the lower the unemployment rate. Compare earnings and unemployment by education level in 2017 with the overall unemployment rate of 3.6%.

Median weekly earnings (in dollars) and unemployment rate (in percent) byeducational attainment, 2017

Educational attainment	Median weekly earnings	Unemployment rate
Doctoral degree	$1,743	1.5%
Professional degree	1,836	1.5
Master's degree	1,401	2.2
Bachelor's degree	1,173	2.5
Associate degree	836	3.4
Some college, no degree	774	4.0
High school diploma, no college	712	4.6
Less than a high school diploma	520	6.5
Total	907	3.6

Note: Data are for persons age 25 and over. Earnings are for full-time wage and salary workers.
Source: U.S. Bureau of Labor Statistics, Current Population Survey.

Going to college is important, so how do you pay for it?

Pay Your Own Way

The best way to pay for college is to save money from working and pay as you go.

You may be able to earn some extra money through side hustles (such as driving for Lyft/Uber, selling items on Etsy, tutoring, and babysitting) and paid internships. Living at home will conserve money. Having roommates to split bills with would also help.

Some employers may offer tuition reimbursement.

Saving does not start a week before you enroll, it must be done on a consistent basis. For help in saving money, see Chapter 1: Budget Your Way to Financial Security and Chapter 6: Save Money.

Financial Aid

Every student, even those who do not think they will qualify, should complete the Free Application for Federal Student Aid (FAFSA). You can find the form at https://studentaid.ed.gov/sa/fafsa. Not only financial aid but also some scholarships are disbursed based on this application. Be sure to file by the deadlines!

Work Study

Work study provides part-time employment to students while they are enrolled in school. It is available to both full-time and part-time students and is administered by schools participating in a Federal Work-Study Program.

Check with your school's financial aid office to find out if your school participates. It is a great way to get involved on campus while making some money.

Grants

Unlike student loans, grants do not require repayment. They can be awarded toward specific educational expenses, specific types of students, or general purpose. Unlike scholarships, which are typically awarded on the basis of academic achievement or athletic, artistic or extracurricular performance, grants are awarded according to financial need. You may qualify to receive a grant by completing the FAFSA.

One grant worth mentioning is the Federal Pell Grant Program. This program provides need-based grants to low-income undergraduate and certain postbaccalaureate students with the goal of promoting access to colleges and universities. You may receive up to twelve semesters of Pell Grants.

You can also find student- and subject-specific grants (e.g., female students, low-income students, students with disabilities, veterans, STEM, underrepresented students). Check with your college financial aid office or do some internet research to see if there are grants that you may qualify for.

Scholarships

A scholarship is an award of financial aid for a student to further their education. Scholarships are awarded based upon various criteria, which usually reflect the values and purposes of the donor or founder of the award. Scholarship money is not required to be repaid.

While scholarships may have a financial need component, many rely on other criteria.

Academic scholarships typically use a minimum grade point average or standardized test score, such as the ACT or SAT, to select recipients.

Athletic scholarships are based on athletic performance of a student and are generally used as a tool to recruit high-performing athletes for their school's athletic teams.

Merit scholarships can be based on a number of criteria, including performance in a particular school subject or even club participation or community service.

Throughout the year, each campus receives announcements about scholarship opportunities. The focus of each scholarship is different. Some scholarships require good grades, some require financial need, and some are awarded to students who are majoring in certain areas. Contact your college financial aid office or do some internet research to see if there are any scholarships you may qualify for.

Action Items

- Complete the FAFSA, even if you don't think you will meet the requirements for aid; you may be surprised!
- See if you qualify for any campus work-study jobs.
- Apply for any grants and scholarships you may be able to get.
- Review Chapter 3: Student Loans to see if a loan is right for you.

CHAPTER 3

STUDENT LOANS

Student debt is a product that has been sold to us with such repetition and intensity that most people believe they can't live without.

—Unknown

College is part of the American Dream. It shouldn't be part of a financial nightmare for families.

—Barbara Mikuski

Give a man an education and he will build a new world, but give a man a loan and you can own that man forever.

—Unknown

As discussed in Chapter 2: How to Pay for College, there are many ways to pay for college. This chapter discusses some of the ways you can obtain a loan.

Is a Student Loan Worth It?

It's not an easy question to ask yourself, but it's one worth considering: Will the amount of money you're likely to make when you finish college be enough to pay off your student loan debt?

Before you sign on to any loan, student or otherwise, do the math. Find out how long it will take you to pay back that loan at the average salary you will likely earn from your job, and think about whether you're willing to be in debt for that long. Loans are not free, so be sure to include the interest you will be paying!

Federal vs. Private Student Loans

Student loans generally come in one of two forms: federal/state (government funded) or private (individual lenders like credit unions or banks). Government student loans tend to come with incentives like fixed interest rates and the ability to restructure payments based on income.

Private loans come in a variety of forms. With a little research, you may be able to find a private loan with lower interest rates and more favorable terms.

Time Matters

When it comes to repaying your student and other loans, the faster you agree to pay off your debt, the more you'll pay per month. By paying the loans off quicker, you will be spending less in interest over the life of the loan. On the other hand, if you decide to make smaller payments toward your debt over a longer period of time, you will pay significantly more interest.

Know Your Grace Period

The grace period—that is, how long you can wait after graduation before your loan payments start—vary, so be sure to find out when your first payment will be due. A grace period can be helpful if you need time to get a job and earn some money before making payments. Many federal student loans offer a grace period, but most private student loans do not.

Refinancing Your Loan

There are two ways to modify your student loans, depending on whether they are federal or private. These processes are often confused, but they're very different.

Federal student loan consolidation combines multiple federal loans into a single loan through the Department of Education. You may do this to become eligible for some federal loan repayment programs. Keep in mind that federal consolidation won't lower your interest rate but might lower your monthly payments by extending the time you pay them off. This means, of course, you will end up paying more for the use of the money.

Student loan refinancing, which is also called private student loan consolidation, is done through a private lender. If you qualify, you might save money by getting a lower interest rate and a longer payment period.

Here are some reasons to consider refinancing your loan:

- *Your income is secure.* You, or your co-signer, will generally need a credit score at least in the high 600s to qualify for student loan refinancing. Without secure income and credit, you probably will not be able to refinance. Before applying, check out Chapter 4: Other Loans for tips on obtaining a loan.
- *Your loan interest rate is high.* If your interest rate is already low, there is no reason to consider refinancing. If your rate is higher than what you can get by refinancing, doing so is certainly an option.
- *You may qualify for federal loan repayment programs.* Keep in mind that you may end up paying more in the long run, since the payment period is frequently extended.

- *You don't qualify for federal loan forgiveness.* If you qualify, there is no need to refinance a loan that will be forgiven!
- *You recently started paying off the loans.* If you are close to the end of repaying your loans, there is no reason to extend the payments further in the future. The earlier in the loan term, the more you will benefit from refinancing.

Forbearance and Deferment

You may need to take breaks in payments from time to time; forbearance and deferment can help in these situations. Forbearance allows you to either stop making loan payments or have them reduced for a certain amount of time (interest will likely still be charged). Deferment allows you to stop making payments and pay later, usually with interest charged for that period of time. Different lenders have different policies.

Consequences If You Don't Pay

If you fail to pay your student loan, you probably won't find a team of armed U.S. Marshals at your front door, but it's still a very bad idea to ignore that debt. Most student loans are guaranteed by the federal government, and the feds have powers that debt collectors can only dream about. It probably won't be as bad as armed marshals at your door, but it could get very unpleasant.

When your loan payment is ninety days overdue, it is officially delinquent. This will be reported to all three major credit bureaus, and your credit rating will be hit. That means that next time you apply for credit, you may be denied or have to pay higher interest rates charged to risky borrowers. Potential employers often check the credit ratings of applicants and use it as a measure of your character, as do cell phone service providers, who may deny you the service contract you want. Utility companies may demand a security deposit from customers they don't consider creditworthy. A prospective landlord might reject your application.

When your payment is 270 days late, it is officially in default. The financial institution you owe the money to refers the problem to a collection agency, who will do its best to make you pay up. Debt collectors also may tack on fees, in addition to the interest you already owe, to cover the cost of collecting the money.

It may be years down the road before the federal government gets involved, but when they do, their powers are considerable. They can take your tax refund and apply it to your outstanding debt. Or they can garnish your paycheck, meaning they will contact your employer and arrange for a portion of your salary to be sent directly to the government.

Student loans are not dischargeable in bankruptcy. Unlike most other debts that can be forgiven if you declare bankruptcy, student loans will be with you forever.

Consider Other Loans

Student loans can be an important part of your financial plan and help pay for college. But they may not be the only loan option you have. Be sure to check out Chapter 4: Other Loans for more information.

Action Items

- Consider if you really need a loan or can pay for college a different way, perhaps by working or getting assistance from relatives.
- Look into both federal and private loans to see which is best for you.
- Understand what you are getting into, including the term of the loan and any grace period.
- If you already have loans, consider refinancing them only if refinancing saves you significant money.
- Know the consequences of not repaying student loans!

CHAPTER 4

OTHER LOANS

Debt is like any other trap, easy enough to get into, but hard enough to get out of.

—Henry Wheeler Shaw

Some debts are fun when you are acquiring them, but none are fun when you pay them.

—Ogden Nash

If you would know the value of money, try to borrow some.

—Benjamin Franklin

Applying for a loan requires a lot of research—not just on loan specifics but your needs and wants as well! Loans make some of our biggest life decisions possible, so it's crucial to be realistic about your goals, your financial situation and your future.

Loan Terminology

APR: The APR or Annual Percentage Rate is the yearly (annual) cost of your loan (your interest rate plus any additional fees).

Interest Rate: The amount charged to you for the use of the loaned money. It is typically expressed as a percentage.

Payment: The amount you promise to pay, usually monthly, until the loan is paid off.

Principal: The amount of money you borrow.

Term: The time period in which you agree to pay back your loan.

Types of Interest Rates

Fixed Rate: The interest rate and payments stay the same throughout the loan term.

Variable Rate: The interest rate and payment can change throughout the loan, based on an index chosen by the lender. If the index goes up or down, so does your interest rate and monthly payment.

Preparing for a Loan

What does your credit score look like? Credit scores play a big role in loan approval and your interest rate. If your score is low, it's a good idea to work on it before applying for a loan.

If you want to verify what has been reported, go to https://www.annualcreditreport.com/index.action. You may also want to review tips on how to improve your credit at https://www.credit.com/credit-repair/how-to-improve-credit-score/.

What does your budget look like? Before signing a loan agreement, you need to have a clear idea of your monthly expenses. This will let you know what repayment terms you can afford.

Who are you dealing with? Lenders come in many shapes and sizes, including large national banks, local credit unions and payday lenders. Look closely at your lender's history and reputation.

Ask questions. Asking hypothetical questions such as, "What happens if I miss a monthly payment?" is a great way to get practical information.

Take your time. Taking out a loan is an important decision, so give it time. You should never feel pressured to agree to something on the spot.

Car Loans: Buy or Lease

Even though two cars may be identical, the method of financing them are very different.

Leasing is sort of like renting a car for a fixed period of time. When you lease, you're paying for the value of the car you use up during your term, plus interest. What's left is known as the residual value of the vehicle.

- You lease a car for a fixed term, typically two to four years.
- An initial deposit is often required.
- You make monthly payments to continue using the vehicle.
- At the end of the lease, you give back the vehicle.

Financing is buying a car through a loan. You can finance a car through the dealership or through a financial institution, like a credit union.

- Loan terms can range from three to seven years.
- An initial deposit is often required.
- Your monthly payments go toward repaying the balance of the loan plus the interest.
- At the end of the loan, you own the car.

Pros and Cons of Buying vs. Leasing

	Buy	Lease
Ownership	You own the vehicle. You can keep, sell or trade it in at any time.	You don't own the vehicle. You must return it at the end of the lease and get a new one.
Payments	Since you own the vehicle, monthly payments will be higher. This can be reduced by having a longer loan term.	Monthly payments are usually 30% to 60% lower than buying.
Customization	If you want to make changes to the look or performance of your car, you can do whatever you want to your vehicle.	Changes can only be done with prior approval. New sound systems or other modifications are usually not allowed.
Mileage	You own the car, so you can drive across the country if you want.	Typical limits are 10,000 miles per year; there is a charge if you go over your limit. Most people drive 15,000 per year and pay a penalty.
Wear and Tear	It is your car, so there is no additional cost (other than reduced value) for any damage.	Since a leased car is a borrowed car, wear and tear will be held against you and may cost more at the end of your lease.

Action Items

- Take a look at your credit to see if you should clean it up prior to applying for a loan. The better your credit, the better terms you will get on a loan.
- Prior to taking out a loan, consider if you can afford it another way. Or consider not buying it at all.
- For loans you already have, be sure you are making the payments on time. This will save any late fees and improve your credit score.

5 CHAPTER

CREDIT CARDS

If you don't take good care of your credit, then your credit won't take good care of you.

—Tyler Gregory

You cannot escape the responsibility of tomorrow by evading it today.

—Abraham Lincoln

To contract new debts is not the way to pay old ones.

—George Washington

Living life without a credit card can feel like getting by without cable TV. You can function, but you just might feel like you're missing out sometimes. Your credit score says as much, if not more, about you than your social media profiles; credit cards provide the foundation for that score. Without a good credit score, achieving many of the financial goals that are most important to you would be nearly impossible.

Do You Need a Credit Card?

Plusses:

- ✓ Credit cards are more convenient than using cash or a debit card.
- ✓ You can use your credit card statements to track your spending.
- ✓ Credit cards can provide a quick loan if necessary.
- ✓ Some cards have perks, incentives and rewards.
- ✓ It is easier to rent cars and hotel rooms if you have a credit card.
- ✓ Credit cards allow you to build a credit history.

Negatives:

- ✓ Credit cards make it too easy to spend beyond your means.
- ✓ Credit card statements are more paperwork than you are accustomed to.
- ✓ If you carry a balance or miss a payment, there will be fees you have to pay.
- ✓ They charge fees for "conveniences" like cash advances.
- ✓ Credit cards have high interest rates.
- ✓ Improperly used, credit cards can damage your credit history.

Plastic is not always fantastic. In financially irresponsible hands, a credit card can lead you into all types of pitfalls and catastrophes, including bankruptcy. A credit card is an important tool, one you should use wisely to build a solid credit reputation.

Getting a Credit Card

Credit card offers and provisions are not exactly written in plain English. It's basic marketing on the front end, terms on the back (usually in small print).

Credit cards will almost always cost you something; some are costlier than others. Before you even think of applying, ask these key questions:

- What's the interest rate?
- Will I be charged different interest rates for purchases, balance transfers, and cash advances?
- Is there an annual fee, and what else might I have to pay?
- What's the length of the grace period (if any)?

Establish a Usage Plan

The best approach is to pay the entire balance, in full, each month! By carrying a balance, you pay interest and, if you are late, additional fees.

Before You "Transfer Your Balance"

Credit card companies commonly lure you by offering balance transfers at low introductory "teaser" interest rates. Put simply, this means moving your debt from one credit card to another, hoping to eliminate high finance charges and fees. That's all fine and dandy, until you discover that they almost all offer:

- a higher interest rate on new purchases;
- a low introductory interest rate that only applies for a short period of time;
- balance transfer fees; and
- termination fees and retroactive interest charges when you move your debt somewhere else.

Of course, if you pay your card off every month, you will never have a balance to transfer!

Understanding Your Credit Score

What's your credit score? If you don't know, it's a good idea to find out because this simple number can have an important impact on your financial life.

Your credit score is a rating of your creditworthiness, essentially how risky it is to lend you money. Your FICO score—the one most often used—ranges from 300 to 850, with the higher the number, the better. Credit reports are created by three companies—Equifax, Experian and TransUnion—based on several factors:

- Your payment history, including late payments or delinquencies (35% of the score).
- How much you owe as a percent of total credit (30%).
- How long you've had credit (15%).
- The type of credit used (10%).
- The amount of recent credit you have (10%).

Check Your Credit

You have the right to request one free credit report every twelve months from each of the three credit bureaus. You can get these, for free, by going to https://www.annualcreditreport.com/index.action.

These reports will not include your credit score. Some financial institutions will provide you with your credit score for free, so it is usually not necessary to pay somebody to see it. It's a good idea to check your credit reports regularly to be sure they are accurate and to alert the credit bureaus if you find an error or signs of possible identity theft.

Why It Is Important

Whether you are getting a mortgage, financing a car, renting an apartment or getting a new credit card, lenders want to know how well you've used credit in the past to decide whether they should lend you money now. They do this by checking your credit reports and score. If you have a low score or problems showing up on your credit report, you may have trouble finding a lender who will lend to you, you will have to pay a high interest rate to get credit, and you might not be able to rent a house or apartment easily.

Action Items

- Get your credit report, now, from one of the three credit bureaus. Every four months, check another bureau to see that there is nothing that should not be on your report.
- If you find any errors, report them immediately.
- Pay off your credit card balances, in full, every month. If you are a bit behind, make a plan to pay them off as soon as possible.
- If you can't pay the bill, consider if you are using credit wisely and make adjustments to your spending patterns.

6 CHAPTER

SAVE MONEY

Never spend your money before you have earned it.

—Thomas Jefferson

A simple fact that is hard to learn is that the time to save money is when you have some.

—Joe Moore

The quickest way to double your money is to fold it in half and put it in your back pocket.

—Will Rogers

With credit so easy to get, why would anyone want to save money and buy with cash? If you want something, you pull out the plastic and then pay it back with payments. If you can afford the minimum monthly payments, what's the big deal? The unfortunate thing is that this sort of thinking is making people poorer without them even knowing it.

Why You Should Save

Financial Independence

Most people think that "being rich or wealthy" means having financial independence. Calling your own shots, financially speaking, means having the freedom to make choices in your life separate from earning a paycheck.

This may mean being able to take a vacation whenever you want, leaving work and going back to school to switch careers, starting your own business, helping family members, taking on a lesser paying job that is more personally satisfying, or even retiring when you want to rather than working because you *have* to.

Financial independence isn't the same as being rich, but not having to depend on receiving a weekly paycheck can make you feel rich beyond your wildest dreams!

Save 50%

If you normally charge all of your purchases on your credit card and then don't pay the credit cards in full every month, you are probably paying at least 50% more for everything you buy because of added interest and finance charges. If you are relying on your credit cards to afford your lifestyle, break that expensive credit habit by saving cash for your purchases instead of charging them.

With money in the bank, you can also buy things when they are on sale and take the time to make better spending choices. For example, you can stockpile nonperishable groceries when they are on sale.

Buy a Home

The bank won't lend you money to buy a house unless you have a down payment. You are not allowed to borrow a down payment, which usually is at least 5%–20% of the purchase price of the house. Only once you have the cash for a down payment will a bank consider lending you the rest. There are all sorts of other costs and fees that you need to pay when you buy a home, so you will need an additional 5% just for those possible expenses. Savings is what will open the door to owning a home. For more information, see Chapter 11: Buying a Home.

Buy a Car

When you want or need to buy a new car, you may need to have a down payment in order to get a car loan at a reasonable interest rate. You could, of course, "borrow" the money from your credit card, but at 20+%, how is that getting you ahead? Car leases have a smaller monthly payment but still cost you something—and it usually is a lot more than buying.

The best thing you can do is save up as large a down payment as you can afford, and then consider your options. Maybe buying a quality used car rather than a new one will be what it takes to ultimately get you the vehicle you want. See Chapter 4: Other Loans for tips on buying a car.

Get out of Debt

Credit cards are never going to get paid off if you have to keep using them for every "emergency" that comes along. Even if you are an awesome planner, half of us experience at least one totally unexpected expense each year (and half of those will be unexpected car trouble).

Before you start aggressively paying off your credit cards, you should save some money in a reserve fund. When unexpected things come up, you can pay them out of your reserve fund rather than putting the expense on your credit cards.

Annual Expenses

If you want to have a good, relatively stress-free financial life, you need to save for annual expenses. This may include money for gifts, vacations, vehicle maintenance, minor home repairs, fixing appliances, property and income tax. It can be tempting to refinance a mortgage to pay off debt or to use a line of credit to pay off high-interest credit cards, but it is dangerous to endlessly put expenses on credit without actually paying them off. The best way to manage these types of expenses is to save for them in advance. This will not only save you money, but it will also give you peace of mind. See Chapter 1: Budget Your Way to Financial Security for tips on preparing a budget.

Unforeseen Expenses

What will you do if your car needs some major repairs? Do you have $500 to $3,000 on hand? What if you are living in a building that leaks? It is much better to anticipate a worst-case scenario and have some money saved.

As much as we hope that emergencies won't happen, they do. A family member can develop a health issue, you might need to make an emergency trip, you may have a car accident or breakdown, or you may have to fly to a loved one's funeral. Any of these emergencies can be expensive.

You Could Lose Your Job or Get Hurt

In good times, everyone thinks that their job is secure, but in bad times, many begin to realize that stuff can happen to anyone. You could suddenly lose your job, your business could dry up, or you might get injured or become too sick to work. Do you have enough savings to tide you over, or will you be living on credit?

Living on credit during a time like this can quickly make a bad situation worse. Minimum payments become higher and higher until they are unaffordable, and credit limits no longer are allowed to increase. When you finally do get some income, what used to be enough doesn't get you by because you have all these new debt payments to make. So now you actually need more income than before because you'll need to pay down these debts.

To Have a Good Life

You have nothing to lose by saving and only a happier future to gain.

Simple Strategies to Save

OK, you should save. But how?

Start Small

Put aside some money every paycheck. It does not have to be a lot, but over time, it will add up. If, for example, you can save $10 per week, do it. If you work overtime or don't seem to need the money right now, you can always add to that minimum amount. In any case, promise yourself to never save less than the minimum.

Set up an Automatic Investment Plan

Instead of taking your whole paycheck, have some of it go automatically to a savings or investment account. This makes it difficult for you to spend what you don't see, and your savings will increase faster.

Bank Your Raises

Congratulations, you got a raise. Instead of spending the additional amount, add the newfound wealth to your savings. You can live just as well as before but will suddenly have a nest egg building up.

Contribute to Your Retirement Savings Plan

If your employer has a 401(k) or 403(b) plan, contribute the maximum; even better, if they match your contribution, you earn money right away.

No retirement plan? No problem. You may be eligible for an Individual Retirement Account (IRA). Add to this that the amount you set aside in any retirement plan or an IRA is not currently taxed and this is sort of a "no-brainer". See Chapter 13: Retirement for retirement tips.

"Round Up" Your Payments

If you are making mortgage payments, adding a bit to the principal every month will enable you to pay it off quicker. Plus, if the interest rate is, say, 5%, you immediately earn 5% on your money. Not bad for putting money into your pocket.

Pay Off Your Credit Cards

Credit card issuers don't want you to pay the balances off; they would rather you incur interest and late fees. Make it a goal to not pay the minimum amount; pay the entire amount due each month and never pay interest.

Reinvest Dividends

If you have any investments that generate dividends, instead of taking the cash, have the dividends reinvested. Not only will you usually get a discount when purchasing the stock, but it is an easy way to compound your earnings and make even more money.

Don't Forget about Taxes

It is easy to forget about your partner—the government! Keep your withholding amount at a level that you expect to "break even" when you file your taxes, so you neither owe much nor get a huge refund. Also, take advantage of tax breaks like the home mortgage deduction, education, child care and dependent credits. Chapter 7: Income Taxes has information about how taxes work.

Separate the "Wants" from the "Needs"

Look at where you are spending your money and think about how necessary each of the expenditures is. Is Starbucks really necessary every day, or how about just once a week? Is a new purse that important, or will the old one do? Is a new car really necessary, or can you repair your current one and get a couple years more use out of it?

Action Items

- Commit to saving money. Unless you make a conscious effort, it won't happen.
- Start small and see how it works.
- Find out if your employer has any sort of retirement savings plan, and if so, sign up. If you are already in a plan, see if you can increase your contribution. If you are not covered, consider opening up an IRA.
- Review the other tips, and see how many of them you can put into action.

7 CHAPTER

INCOME TAXES

Taxes are the price we pay for civilization.

—Oliver Wendell Holmes, 1930

Death, taxes and childbirth! There's never any convenient time for any of them.

—Margaret Mitchell, *Gone with the Wind*, 1936

Income tax returns are the most imaginative fiction being written today.

—Herman Wouk

You're working. Congratulations, you have partners: the federal, state and city governments. Welcome to the world of taxes.

What are Taxes?

Taxes are fees charged to individuals or businesses on income, activities or products by federal, state and local governments. In exchange, you receive something provided by the government, like roads, schools and public health services.

When you look at your paycheck, the total amount you earned isn't the same as the amount you take home. Some of what you earn goes toward taxes: federal income, state income, Social Security, Medicare and local taxes are deducted from your paycheck.

But that is not all. In addition to the payroll taxes just listed, other taxes we pay include sales taxes (on purchases) and property taxes (when you own real estate).

Taxes provide money for the government to operate and provide services to us. While taxes lower the amount of the income you take home, we also need what taxes pay for—education, police and fire protection, roads and parks, to name a few. What would we do if everybody had to personally arrange and pay for these, and other, services?

In this chapter we will focus on income taxes.

Taxable Income

What do I pay tax on? Wages, commissions, interest paid to you from a bank, and money you make when you sell an asset are all forms of *income*. You pay tax on your income.

Gifts and loans are not income. Gifts might be taxable to the person who gave you the money but not to you, the recipient. Loans have to be paid back; you do not pay tax when you get the loan and, logically, you do not get to deduct the amount when you pay it back.

Deductions

You get to deduct from your income certain exemptions and deductions or, as they are commonly called, "write offs". Those items reduce the total on which you figure your tax. The balance after subtracting those deductions is your *taxable income*. That creates the appeal of "write offs" and "deductions". Those items reduce the total on which you figure your tax.

What are common deductions? Many people have the opportunity to write off the interest paid on their home mortgage, property and income taxes, some medical costs and charitable contributions.

The government gives you a *standard deduction*, which varies every year. If your deductions are more than the standard deduction, you are allowed to write off the extra amount; if your deductions are less, you use the standard deduction instead. Typically, only homeowners have enough write-offs to not have to use the standard deduction.

There are also special rules for business owners and real estate investors, among others.

As Your Income Increases, so Do Your Taxes

The range of income subject to a given tax rate is a *bracket*. Each bracket applies a higher rate to the taxable income that falls in that bracket.

There were seven federal tax brackets in 2018. Here are the brackets for a single taxpayer:

Taxable Income	Rate
Up to $9,255	10%
$9,256 to $38,699	12%
$38,700 to $82,499	22%
$82,500 to $157,499	24%
$157,500 to $199,999	32%
$200,000 to $499,999	35%
$500,000 or more	37%

Each tier of your income is taxed at the rate for that tier, or bracket. So, if you are single, your first $9,255 in taxable income triggers a tax at 10%, or $926. If you had a total of $25,000 in taxable income, you pay tax of 12% on all the income over $9,255. Doing the math, your total tax on $25,000 in taxable income would be $2,815 ($926 tax at the 10% rate + $1,889 tax at the 12% rate).

The *marginal tax rate* is the percentage of tax on the last dollar you make. Looking at our previous example, your marginal tax rate would be 12%, since that is the highest bracket. If you made $38,700 your marginal tax rate would be 22%.

The *effective tax rate* is the percentage of tax on your taxable income. In the previous example, the effective tax rate would be 11.3% ($2,815 tax ÷ $25,000 taxable income).

Tax Credits

To encourage certain behaviors, the government offers *tax credits*. For example, to use less fossil fuels, the government encourages us to install solar panels on our homes. If you do so, you may have earned a tax credit.

A tax credit is better than a deduction. A tax credit directly decreases the amount of taxes you pay, dollar-for-dollar. A deduction, while still good, only lowers the taxable income, so your savings is whatever your marginal rate is. For example, if you have a $3,000 expense for solar panels and your marginal rate is 22%, you save $660 with that deduction. With a tax credit, the amount is subtracted directly from the amount of tax you owe the government, so you would save the entire $3,000.

Common tax credits include the following:

- *Child care credit.* Based on your income and the amount you pay for child care, this amount, up to a certain limit, is subtracted directly from the tax you owe.
- *Earned income credit.* If you don't make much money, you can take the earned income tax credit. In some cases, this can be refunded to you even if you pay little or no tax.
- *Education credits.* Because the government wants to encourage us to expand our knowledge and skills after high school, they've

developed some education tax credits and deductions to help offset the expense of higher education.

Tax Withholding

Tax law requires that you pay this year's taxes in advance, even though the final tax return is not due until April 15th of the following year. Employers are required to *withhold* your estimated taxes from each paycheck. You, however, get to tell them how much tax you expect to owe.

Internal Revenue Service (IRS) *Form W-4* includes a worksheet where you calculate the amount of tax that matches your situation. This produces an approximation of what you'll owe. Your employer uses this to figure how much tax to withhold from each check.

Approximating your taxes is tricky. Withhold too little, and you not only owe taxes but also might have to pay a penalty with your return for not having paid enough in advance. Withhold too much, and you get a refund. Most people like to get refunds, as it provides a nice "bonus" that was not expected.

Doing Your Taxes

If you are new to the tax world, your financial life is probably fairly simple. Take the time to learn how to prepare your own tax returns while things aren't too complicated. There is free tax advice available through the IRS and most state websites as well as many types of easy-to-use commercial tax software. If you have a more complex tax situation, with investments or a business or rental property, it is wise to engage a CPA or tax preparer to help you.

No matter how you decide to handle your taxes, recordkeeping is critical. Accurate, timely documentation will allow you to minimize the income taxes you pay.

In case you are wondering, don't even think about cheating (not declaring all of your income or claiming false deductions or credits).

Despite what you hear, not everybody does it. If you are caught, the penalties can be huge.

Finally

The U.S. tax code has about four million words, which comes out to about nine thousand pages. There are also tax laws for most of the states. If you do not feel comfortable learning the nuances of the law, don't be shy about asking for help.

Action Items

- If you are working, take a look at your Form W-4 to see if it reflects your current financial situation.
- If you normally get a big refund (or owe a lot of tax), adjust your Form W-4.
- If you have a simple tax situation, consider preparing your own tax returns and having somebody review them.
- No matter if you prepare your returns or have a professional do so, before signing them, review the returns and understand every item. Remember, *you* are responsible for what is on the returns and are signing them under penalty of perjury.

8 CHAPTER

IDENTITY THEFT

In 2018, 16.7 million people—one in every fifteen Americans—were victims of identity theft. Which means, yes, it can happen to you.

Young adults (ages eighteen to twenty-four) are one of the groups most susceptible to identity theft, with 29% of identity theft reports coming from this age group.

California led the country with over 55,000 cases of identity fraud. Only Michigan and Florida had more complaints per 100,000 people.

Identity Theft and Identity Fraud Defined

Identity theft and identity fraud are types of crimes in which someone wrongfully obtains and uses another person's personal data in some way that involves fraud or deception, typically for economic gain. As you can see, it is a huge problem.

Common Types of Identity Theft and Fraud

Employment or tax-related fraud (34%). A criminal will use someone else's Social Security number and other personal information to get employment or to file an income tax return.

Credit card fraud (33%). The thief uses someone else's credit card or credit card number to make fraudulent purchases.

Phone or utilities fraud (13%). The criminal uses another person's personal information to open a wireless phone or utility account.

Bank fraud (12%). The fraudster uses someone else's personal information to take over an existing bank account or to open a new account in another name.

Loan or lease fraud (7%). A borrower or a lessee uses someone else's information to obtain a loan or lease.

Government documents or benefits fraud (7%). The criminal uses stolen personal information to obtain government benefits or medical services.

Identity Theft or Fraud Techniques

Shoulder surfing. In public places, criminals might engage in "shoulder surfing" (watching you from a nearby location as you punch in your credit card number). They also are skilled at listening in on your conversations as you give out personal information over the telephone.

Dumpster diving. Criminals might look in your trash for preapproved credit card applications that have not been torn up. Once they find the envelopes, they try to activate the cards for their use without your knowledge.

Stealing your mail. If your mail is delivered to a place where others have access to it, criminals may simply intercept and redirect your mail to another location.

Letting your guard down. Responding to a "spam" e-mail message or phone call that promises something and requests identifying data is an easy way for a thief to take over your identity. Seventy percent of identity fraud reported incidents started with a telephone call!

What They Do with Your Information

With a small bit of identifying information about you, a criminal can take over your identity to conduct a wide range of crimes. For example:

- *False applications for loans and credit cards.* They apply for a credit card or loan in your name, buy a bunch of stuff, and disappear before you even know you have been taken advantage of.
- *Withdrawals from bank accounts.* They simply take most of the money from your bank account.
- *Use of online accounts.* They use online accounts to steal from your bank account or make purchases in your name.
- *Obtaining goods and having them shipped to another address.* Crooks use your credit card or other personal information and then have the stuff sent to another address, where it is promptly sold.

Ways to Avoid Identity Theft

- Make a list of all of your credit and debit cards, even those you don't carry in your wallet.
  - Include account numbers and the names and emergency phone numbers of each issuer.
  - Store this in a secure place that's quickly accessible to you.
  - Don't keep the list in your wallet!
- If possible, don't let your credit or debit card out of your sight when you pay for something.
- Don't carry your birth certificate or Social Security card in your wallet.
- If possible, install a locked mailbox to prevent mail theft.

- When dining out, keep your purse or wallet secure.
- Never let anyone see you type in your personal identification number (PIN).
- Don't write your PIN on your ATM card (yes, people do that!).
- Shred preapproved credit card or loan applications before you throw them in the trash.
- Check your bank statements at least monthly.
- Order a copy of your credit report three times a year. You can get free reports at https://www.annualcreditreport.com/index.action.
- Don't give out your Social Security, credit card or bank account number to anyone who calls you.
- Avoid using Wi-Fi in public places like Starbucks. And be conscious of who is sitting nearby.
- Be wary of unsolicited email and watch out for links that are fake. If you happen to click on one of them and realize that it is fraudulent, immediately exit the program, and if possible, restart your computer.

What If It Happens to You?

- Check your homeowners or renter's insurance policy to see if you are covered. See Chapter 9: Insurance for tips on insurance.
- Call the companies where you know the fraud occurred. Change user names, passwords, and PINs for all of your accounts.
- Place a fraud alert and get your credit reports.
- Report identity theft to the Federal Trade Commission (FTC). Go to https://identitytheft.gov or call 1-877-438-4338. Based on the information you enter, they will create an Identity Theft Report and personal recovery plan.

Action Items

- Check your credit report. If there is anything suspicious, immediately investigate it.
- Update your computer's virus protection program.
- Re-read the suggestions in this chapter to avoid identity theft—and follow them!

PART 2

ON YOUR OWN

As you continue your life, there are many things to consider. Perhaps you will be living away from home; how does that work? And where do you even begin when it comes to insurance?

In this section, you will become familiar with these topics and get some tips to help you start your financial life on the right foot. As you review each chapter, be sure to take the "action steps" right away, while they are on your mind.

If you have not already done so, review Chapters 1 through 8 for additional basic knowledge:

Enjoy becoming financially savvy!

9 CHAPTER

INSURANCE

Fun is like life insurance; the older you get, the more it costs.

—Kin Hubbard

Without health insurance, getting sick or injured could mean going bankrupt, going without needed care, or even dying needlessly.

—Jan Schakowsky

There are worse things in life than death. Have you ever spent an evening with an insurance salesman?

—Woody Allen

What Is Insurance?

Imagine this:

You sprain your ankle playing soccer and have to go to the emergency room, and you are charged $2,000 for the visit.

You are backing up and accidentally scrape the entire driver's side of your neighbor's car, causing $2,500 of damage.

You come home to find the front door unlocked and your stuff missing.

All of these are unexpected costs that many people don't have the money to pay. Thus, the concept of insurance was invented in the twelfth century. Simply put, *insurance* allows businesses and individuals to pool their money to protect them against unexpected risks (like spraining your ankle or hitting your neighbor's car).

You purchase insurance by paying a *premium*—the cost of the insurance. The premium can be annual (once a year), semi-annual (every six months) or monthly; the frequency of payment depends on the type of insurance and the company.

When you pay your premium, the company issues an *insurance policy*. This is an agreement that says what the company will pay should you have certain losses.

In order to keep the premium down, most policies have a *deductible*. This is the amount of the loss that you pay before the company pays the rest.

Insurance does not pay an infinite amount. Every type of insurance has *policy limits*, which is the maximum amount the company will pay for the specific loss.

Where You Purchase Insurance

An insurance agent represents one or several companies. If you like personal attention and the ability to have somebody shop around for the best coverage, this is a good option.

Directly from the company. Many companies do not use agents and write the policy directly. When you do an internet search for policies, this option may pop up. Many times, but not always, this sort of company will be a bit less costly since they do not have to pay an agent a commission.

Check out the Company

Not all insurance companies are the same! As with many businesses (and make no mistake about it, insurance companies are businesses), some are more stable than others. It would be a shame if, after paying your premiums, the company went out of business and they were not able to pay your claim. And, yes, it does happen.

Prior to purchasing a policy, or to just check out the one(s) you currently are using, you should look at their financial stability at A.M. Best Co.

There are numerous types of insurance that individuals (and businesses) can purchase. As you review them, think about how each of these types of policies might protect you, not only now but also in the future.

Auto Insurance

Auto insurance protects you against unforeseen costs connected with driving and owning a car, truck or motorcycle. There are essentially four basic types of auto insurance:

Liability insurance covers damages for injuries and property damage to others.

Collision insurance covers damage to your car.

Comprehensive insurance covers damage to your car for incidents other than an accident, such as vandalism.

Uninsured motorist insurance covers you against hit-and-run drivers and somebody who does not have enough insurance to cover the damage.

In many states, including California, you must have auto insurance in order to own and drive an automobile. Note that the required coverage is minimal and does not pay for much in case of an incident. Many people elect to purchase more insurance in case of an unexpectedly big loss.

Action Items

- Find out if you have auto insurance. If you drive and do not, arrange for some immediately!

- Find out what company your policy is with. Do you have an agent, or is the policy written directly through the company?
- What is your coverage? If something happens, will that be enough?
- Investigate what your deductible is. Consider raising the deductible so the premium will be less, but don't choose too high a deductible that you cannot afford to pay if you have an accident or claim.

Health Insurance

Health insurance provides preventive services (like an annual physical) as well as protection against unforeseen medical costs.

Health insurance is unique in that you have not only an annual (rather than a per-incident) deductible but also a *co-pay*. For example, let's say you have a policy with a $500 deductible and 20% co-pay for procedures. If you sprain an ankle and the cost of treatment is $2,000, you will pay the $500 deductible plus 20% of the rest (20% x $1,500, or $300). Instead of paying the $2,000 bill, if you have insurance your total responsibility is only $800. In addition, many companies have additional discounts with physicians and hospitals, which reduce the cost even more.

There are many different types of health insurance, but the two most common are:

(1) *Health Maintenance Organization* (HMO). These are networks that use the same physicians, hospitals and other services. They are usually the least costly since the providers have incentives to keep costs down.

(2) *Preferred Provider Organization* (PPO). A physician or hospital agrees to a certain fee structure. If you use a provider in their network, you get a discount and lower co-pay; if you want to use another provider, your cost, including the co-pay,

will be higher. The advantage of this sort of insurance is that you can use any doctor, but if they are outside the network, it will cost you more.

One common misconception is that health insurance covers everything. Unless you have an accident, it will not pay for vision services (eye exams, glasses or contact lenses) or dental work (exams, fillings and orthodontia). You can get insurance for these, but the benefits are usually not worth the cost.

Because health insurance is so important, in addition to the usual places you can get insurance (agent and direct), there are three major government programs to help:

- *Medicare* is insurance that covers most people age sixty-five and older. It is important to sign up at or very close to your sixty-fifth birthday or coverage becomes more expensive.
- *Medi-Cal* is insurance for many low-income residents of California. Most other states have similar plans.
- *CoveredCalifornia* is available to California residents whose income is too high to qualify for Medi-Cal but are otherwise not covered. Some other states have similar plans.

Many people are covered under a health plan by their employer.

Action Items

- Find out if you have health insurance. If you are twenty-six years old or less, you may be covered under your parent's policy.
- Find out what type of policy you have and who the insurance company is.
- Discover what your deductible and co-pay responsibilities are.
- Take advantage of the preventative care feature for a free annual physical exam.

Disability Insurance

Disability insurance provides protection if you are disabled and unable to work. If you are employed in California, you may be covered by the California State Disability Plan (CASDI) or a similar, employer-based, plan. This pays for not only short-term disability but also family leave. Some employers also have a supplemental disability plan.

There are essentially two types of disability insurance policies available:

(1) *Short-term.* This is designed to help while you are recovering from an illness or accident, and in some cases, pregnancy.
(2) *Long-term.* If you are unable to work for an extended period of time, the policy will pay you benefits. Most long-term policies have strict definitions as to what qualifies as a disability.

If you are employed in California, CASDI is deducted from your paycheck (currently about 1% of your pre-tax salary). If you are self-employed, you can elect to cover yourself through this plan by paying a quarterly premium.

If you purchase a disability policy, there are various factors that impact the cost—primarily your age, health and the amount you will receive per month.

Action Items

- If you are employed in California, look at your most recent paycheck to verify that you are covered under CASDI.
- Consider a long-term policy to help out if a member of your family is suddenly unable to work. This is a competitive market, so an internet search will probably yield excellent results.

Life Insurance

Life insurance provides a payment upon the death of an individual. There are basically two types of life insurance:

(1) *Term insurance* pays a benefit if the insured person dies within the policy period.
(2) *Whole life insurance* pays the benefit as long as you pay the premium. In addition, these policies generally provide an investment component and cash value.

Life insurance is occasionally provided by an employer but is more commonly sold directly to individuals by an agent. Typically, the younger you are and better health you have, the less expensive the policy will be. Keep in mind that insurance is just that, insurance, not an investment, so term insurance is usually a good (and much more inexpensive) way to go.

Who needs life insurance?

- A family with one spouse who works and the other stays at home. Many people are surprised that the stay-at-home spouse is the one who should be insured!
- A family with young children who want to have funds for college in case one or both of the parents die.
- Anybody who wants to leave something to others when they die.
- Wealthy people who do estate planning.

Action Items

- Find out if you have life insurance, either at work or purchased individually.
- Consider if life insurance is appropriate for you.
- If you already have life insurance, see if there is still a need for it (are the kids out of school, do you have other assets, is it necessary to spend your hard-earned money just to leave your heirs something)?

Long-Term Care Insurance

Long-term care insurance provides funds in case you have a serious long-term care need, like a stroke or Alzheimer's. This insurance pays a daily amount for things like a nursing home or in-home care. It may be hard to believe, but about 40% of the population will need some sort of long-term care at some point their life!

This insurance is sold through agents and on the internet; in addition, some employers offer it. The premium is based on these risk factors:

- *Age.* The younger you start the policy, the less expensive it will be.
- *Coverage.* The more you want per day, the more the policy will cost.
- *Term.* Some policies are for a short period (three to five years), while others are for a lifetime. Obviously, the longer the term, the more expensive the policy.
- *Inflation coverage.* Is the benefit always the same, even twenty years from now, or will it increase based on the increase in prices?

Action Items

- Find out if you have long-term care insurance, either at work or purchased individually.
- Consider if this insurance is appropriate for you. If you or a member of your family needed short- or long-term care, would you be able to afford it?
- Shop around for the least expensive premium and an insurance company that will be around should you have to use the policy.

Casualty Insurance

Casualty insurance protects you from various types of unforeseen events:

- *Property insurance* covers you if your home is damaged from things like a fire or a car driving through the front door.
- *Liability Insurance* covers you if somebody injures themselves on your property, like slipping on your driveway or a dog bite.
- *Renters insurance* covers your property if it is stolen plus provides liability protection in the event somebody is hurt in your house or apartment.
- *Earthquake insurance* provides coverage in case of an earthquake.

Coverage and availability depend on where you live, how old your house is and many other factors. As with all other insurance, the cost varies based on what you are insuring, the company and the deductible you choose.

Action Items

- If you own a house, find out who carries your homeowner's insurance. Take a look at the policy to see what your coverage and deductible are.
- If you are renting, consider a renter's policy. The premium is usually very affordable, and it will provide you protection you would not otherwise have.
- Shop around for the best premium. This is usually a competitive market, so a bit of research may yield some real cost savings.

Umbrella Insurance

Umbrella insurance is additional liability insurance designed to help protect you from major claims and lawsuits; in other words, it helps protect your assets from a big loss.

Imagine you accidentally drive into your neighbor's living room and the damage is $250,000. If, as is common, your auto liability insurance policy limit is $100,000, you will be on the hook for the additional $150,000. An umbrella insurance policy would pay this additional amount.

Umbrella insurance is usually fairly inexpensive and is encouraged for anybody with any significant amount of assets.

Action Items

- Find out if you have umbrella insurance.
- Consider whether umbrella insurance is appropriate for you. If you or a member of your family has a big loss, would you be able to afford the amount over your current insurance policy limits?
- Shop around for the least expensive premium.

10 CHAPTER

LIVING ON YOUR OWN

College towns are all the same; same burger, different wrapper.
—Sheri Webber, *Devil Went Down: And Hell Came Running*

College life is different, entirely different, like you don't have to get ready and wear that red and crisp blue school uniform and look alike every day. Free to define ourselves with statement attire. Good thing.
—Parul Wadhwa, *The Masquerade*

The people you live with at college, those first roommates often are people you're still friends with the rest of your life.
—Richard Linklater

Many college students have a hard time deciding between living at home or in a dorm or off-campus housing. Some cannot wait to experience dorm life while others are 100% sure that they want to get an apartment or rent a large house with friends.

Finding a Place to Live

Where do you want to live? There are a number of things to keep in mind as you evaluate potential apartments or houses.

- Security, condition of the property and location are the top three. You need to ask your landlord important questions like, "How do I submit my rent payment?" and "How do I report maintenance issues/requests?" If you can, talk with current or future tenants to investigate how the landlord treats them.
- What is important to you? Start by making a list of what features you desire most from your potential apartment or house, then prioritize the list. This will help you focus when looking at housing and comparing your various options. Some concessions will be made, so deciding on the "deal breakers" now will save you time later.
- Be financially wise. Resist the temptation to use student loans for housing you really can't afford. Upscale accommodations are particularly tempting, since they're often constructed near campuses, with really persuasive marketing aimed at students. But resist the urge to sign up.

Roommates

Very few people can afford a house or an apartment on their own. Choose your roommates carefully! If your roommate is unable, or unwilling, to pay their share of the rent or other costs, you potentially can be on the hook for the entire amount.

Consider a roommate agreement. This is a written document designed to get financial and other issues out in the open before you sign a lease and may help avoid conflict later. Who gets which bedroom? How will the community space, including the bathrooms and personal items, be shared? Who will sign up for which utilities? Who will submit rent payments? How will you divide other expenses? A sample agreement can be found at https://students.ucsd.edu/_files/sls/SLS-roommate-agreement-2011.doc

Decide on ground rules. Lay out some rules for things like entertaining, overnight guests, and sharing (or not sharing) groceries. You know what your pet peeves are; make sure to get those out in the open right at the beginning. Choose a roommate who has a similar or complementary living style to you in areas such as privacy, allergies, cleanliness, entertaining and noise.

Up-Front Costs

Even though your lease will not start until sometime in the future, there are a number of up-front costs that you will need to prepare for prior to signing a lease and moving in.

Application Fees, Processing Fees & Credit Check Fees. Most landlords will run a credit check; you pay for that. Additional processing charges may also be added; expect to pay anywhere from $50 to $150.

First Month's Rent. Be prepared to pay your first month's rent at the time you sign your lease.

Security Deposit. The security deposit can from two to three times your monthly rent. If there are no damages for which you are responsible, you should get that security deposit back, sometimes with interest, at the end of your lease. In most cases, you still have to advance the funds.

Signing a Lease

A lease is a legal agreement between you and your landlord. It outlines the commitments to which you are both agreeing. Unless you have a month-to-month lease, which is unusual, the lease will outline a specific timeframe (usually a year) to which this contract applies. You are responsible for paying rent and maintaining the premises during that time.

Understand what you are signing! It is vital that you understand all the terms and conditions of this agreement. Relying on a verbal agreement outside of the lease is dangerous and will only lead to problems later. Get everything in writing, including:

- penalties and obligations, should you need to end your lease early;
- the amount that is charged in case of late rent payments;
- responsibility for damage; and
- subleasing terms.

If you are away for a period of time, like the summer, most leases do not let you sublet your apartment unless you have explicit permission from your landlord. If this is important to you, make sure it is added to your lease.

Be sure that all roommates sign the lease. This puts everybody on the spot for the rent.

One last thing about leases: many landlords use credit reporting agencies. If you are late in paying your rent, your credit will probably get "dinged", which will make it a lot harder to rent the next place to live.

Other Costs to Consider

Paying the rent is just the start. Here are some other costs that you should consider.

Amenities. Many costs, like cable, internet, electricity, garbage and parking, are rolled into the price of some, but not all, housing. Depending on the landlord and type of housing, a lease may include some, all, or none of these items in the rent. You should verify which, if any, of these are included in the rent. If they are not included in the rent, estimate how much each will cost you. They add up!

Eating Habits. Buying groceries and cooking is an economical option, but be realistic about how much you will grocery shop and cook for yourself. Ordering takeout or going out to eat gets expensive fast.

Time Demands. Consider how close you will be to campus (if you are at school), work and family. Think about your schedule, family and extracurricular obligations, jobs you hold, and social life. Try to avoid housing that is so far away that you spend a lot of your life commuting.

Action Items

- Consider what you can afford and who you can get along with in a living arrangement.
- Estimate the up-front costs and see if you are able to pay them.
- Carefully choose the place you will be living and scrutinize the lease.
- Look at not only the rent but also other costs, and be sure that you can afford them.

PART 3

THE REST OF YOUR LIFE

Just because you are finished with your formal education and are on your own, don't think for a second that your learning is over. Sure, you may never have to take another final exam, but you certainly should know what you are doing before purchasing a house. Perhaps you may not want to work forever; how can you set yourself up to retire comfortably? And what if you suddenly are not around? You should think about who you would like to take care of.

In this section you will find information to help you make these and other important financial decisions. As you review each chapter, think about how it affects your personal situation. Be sure to take the "action steps" right away, while they are on your mind.

If you have not already read them, check out these chapters to round out your knowledge:

Chapter 1: Budget Your Way to Financial Security
Chapter 4: Other Loans
Chapter 5: Credit Cards
Chapter 6: Save Money
Chapter 7: Income Taxes
Chapter 10: Living on Your Own

This is just the starting point. Learning never stops!

CHAPTER 11

BUYING A HOME

There is something permanent, and something extremely profound, in owning a home.

—Kenny Guinn

The ache for home lives in all of us. It is a safe place where we can go as we are and not be questioned.

—Maya Angelou

Here lies Walter Fielding. He bought a house, and it killed him.

—Walter Fielding, *The Money Pit*

Buying a home can be nerve-racking, especially if you're a first-time home buyer. Not only is this a huge investment but it is also a very emotional decision. Keeping those emotions in check while wanting a particular house in a certain neighborhood can be challenging.

Estimating What You Can Afford

Traditionally, mortgage lenders have used something known as the 28/36 rule to determine how much of a mortgage you can qualify for. This refers to the two income ratios that are basic guidelines for how much your maximum monthly payment should be.

- The "28" is known as the *front-end ratio*. The "28" means your mortgage payment, including taxes and insurance, shouldn't exceed 28% of your pre-tax income.
- The "36" is called the *back-end ratio*. This means all of your debt, including your mortgage payment, car payments, credit cards, student loans, and similar monthly obligations shouldn't exceed 36% of your pre-tax income.

Some lenders will stretch these limits even further, depending on your credit score, job history and the interest rate—in other words, your risk as a borrower.

In order to get a feel for how much might you qualify for, try this free online calculator https://www.chase.com/personal/mortgage/calculators-resources/affordability-calculator.

Most importantly, whatever number you come up with on this (or any other) calculator will be the *maximum* you can afford. In most cases, that amount will feel very uncomfortable. Remember, you are obligated to make this payment, so stay within what you, not a friend, realtor or random calculator, feel is appropriate.

Mortgage Considerations

When you get a loan on a home, it is called a mortgage. The security for the mortgage is your home; in other words, if you don't pay, the lender can take the home. Here are some other things you should know prior to taking out a mortgage:

Down Payment. Traditionally, it was common for you to put 20% of the purchase price, from your savings, as a down payment. Remember, putting down less than 20% may mean higher costs, including paying an additional amount for private mortgage insurance. On the other hand, even a small down payment can still be hefty.

For example, if your home costs $400,000, you must pay 20% ($80,000) in cash, and the bank will loan you the remainder ($320,000). Many lenders now permit much less than 20%; some first-time home buyer programs allow as little as 3% down. But even a 5% down payment on that $400,000 home is $20,000!

Mortgage Options. There are a lot of mortgage options out there, each with their own combination of pros and cons. If you're struggling to come up with a down payment, check out:

- Conventional mortgages that conform to standards set by the government-sponsored entities. Fannie Mae and Freddie Mac can require as little as 3% down.
- Federal Housing Administration loans permit down payments as low as 3.5%.
- Veterans Affairs loans sometimes do not require a down payment.

If you want the most conservative mortgage payment possible, it is generally wise to take out a thirty-year fixed mortgage. But if you can afford larger monthly payments, you can get a lower interest rate with a fifteen- or twenty-year loan. You may prefer an adjustable-rate mortgage, which means the rate will go up (or down) depending on interest rates in the future. These loans usually have a lower interest rate and payment for the first few years of your mortgage but will adjust based on how much interest rates go up (or down).

Many home buyers get a rate quote from only one lender. It is a competitive market, so many times, with a little shopping around, you can do better. Get at least three quotes to compare rates, fees and the monthly payment. Of course, look for something you feel comfortable you can afford to pay every month!

Preapproval Letter. This letter is given when a lender thoroughly examines your finances and confirms, in writing, how much it's willing to lend you and under what terms. Having a preapproval letter in hand makes you look much more serious to a seller and can give you the upper hand over buyers who haven't taken this step.

Tips When House Shopping

Shopping for a home can be both exciting and frustrating. Here are some tips to keep in mind when considering this important purchase.

Hire the right agent. While you can certainly buy a house yourself, consider hiring an agent who is skilled, motivated and knowledgeable about the area. You'll be working closely with your agent, so it's essential that you find someone you get along with. Remember, the seller, not you, pay the agent's commission, so if the agent does not find you the perfect house, it costs you nothing.

Pick the right type of house and neighborhood. You may start off by assuming you'll buy a single-family home, and that could be ideal if you want a big yard or a lot of room. But if you're willing to sacrifice space for less maintenance and extra amenities, and you don't mind paying a homeowner's association fee, a condo or townhouse could be a better fit. But even if the home is right, the neighborhood could be all wrong. So be sure to do the following:

- Research nearby schools. Even if you don't have kids, schools affect home value.
- Look at local safety and crime statistics. You can do an online search or just stop by the police station.
- Find out where the nearest hospital, pharmacy, grocery store and places you go to regularly are. Are they convenient or a pain to get to?
- Drive through the neighborhood on various days and at different times to check out traffic, noise and activity levels.

Stick to your budget. Start by looking at properties that cost less than the amount you were approved for. Although you can technically afford your preapproval amount, that is the absolute *most* you can afford and doesn't account for other monthly expenses or problems that arise during homeownership, which always seem to happen right after you move in. Buying with a firm budget in mind will also help you know your limitations when it comes time to make an offer.

Check your emotions. In a competitive real estate market with limited inventory, it's possible that you will bid on houses that get multiple offers. When you find a home you love, it's tempting to make a high-priced offer that's sure to win. But don't let your emotions take over. Shopping below your preapproval amount creates some wiggle room for bidding. Stick to your budget to avoid a mortgage payment you can't afford.

Simplified Process of Buying a Home

In order to buy a property, you should know how the process works. They have a lot of industry-specific procedures and words that can be very confusing to the uninitiated.

1. You make an *offer.* If it is accepted by the seller, a contract is signed. The *escrow* process begins.
2. A small deposit is given to an escrow company, who holds your money until the process is completed.
3. You review and sign off on any *disclosures.* These disclosures usually include things like known flaws with the property, prior improvements and repairs, plus potential environmental hazards. Often, a disclosure package is provided by the seller well in advance. If you don't like the disclosures, you can terminate the sale and get your deposit back.
4. You may, or you may hire somebody to, perform an *inspection* of the property. Common inspections include a general, pest, roof, chimney, air conditioning and sewer inspection. Based on the outcome of the inspections, you ask for the seller to:
    - fix the problems;
    - give you money to pay for the problems; or
    - reduce the sale price.

Sellers have three options:
- fix everything discovered in the inspection;
- offer to do some of the repairs; or
- decline to do anything.

Based on this, you can continue to negotiate, accept the seller's position, or, if you cannot work it out, cancel the escrow and get your deposit back.

5. You submit a loan application to a lender, either directly or through a *mortgage broker* (somebody who specializes in finding mortgages). Within three days, the lender sends a *Good Faith Estimate* (GFE) to you that estimates the costs to you (known as *closing costs*). The lender will also request documents plus other disclosures they think are important to your financial situation. Keep in mind: to a lender, anything can happen to your personal financial situation and credit during the escrow process. Thus, you may be asked more than once for the same document, which can be really frustrating.
6. The lender will make an approval decision. If you are approved, they will give you a *loan commitment letter* stating their willingness to fund the mortgage provided certain conditions are met. These conditions usually include an appraisal.
7. An *appraisal*, an independent valuation of the property's value, is ordered by the lender. When you make an offer, there is often an appraisal *contingency*. This means that if the appraisal comes in lower than the purchase price, you can negotiate with the seller, and if negotiations are unsuccessful, the escrow is terminated and you get your deposit back. If the appraisal comes in at or above your purchase price, the lender is satisfied that the purchase price is fair.
8. You purchase homeowners' insurance and send the lender proof that you have it. For tips on insurance, see Chapter 9: Insurance.
9. A *title search* is performed. This is done for the lender to determine if there are any liens or other problems with the seller

that would block you owning the property. Provided the title is *clear*, meaning no problems are discovered, a *title insurance policy* is prepared.

10. You pay the remaining funds due for the down payment, and closing costs, to the escrow company. This is done a few days in advance of when you expect to get the home.
11. The *deed* to the property gets recorded with the appropriate government agency, and the escrow company sends the funds to the appropriate parties.
12. Escrow is closed, and you own the property. You get the keys, and unless indicated differently in the contract, you take possession of the home.

Mistakes to Avoid

Not budgeting for closing costs. In addition to saving for a down payment, you'll need to budget the money required to close your mortgage, which can be between 2% and 5% of your loan amount. You can shop around and compare prices for certain expenses, such as homeowner's insurance, home inspections and title searches. You can also defray costs by asking the seller to pay for a portion of your closing costs or by negotiating the real estate agent's commission.

Not saving enough for after you move in. Once you've saved for your down payment and budgeted for closing costs, you should also set aside funds to pay for what will go inside the house. This includes utility deposits, furniture, appliances, rugs, new paint and any changes you may want to make after moving in. And don't forget about the cost to get your stuff there!

Buying a home for today instead of tomorrow. It's easy to look at properties that meet your current needs, but if you plan to start or expand your family, it may be preferable to buy a larger home that you can grow into. Also, if your job is "iffy" or you plan on moving within a couple of years, buying a house might be better put off until later.

Not negotiating. Most everything is negotiable in the home-buying process. Are there any major repairs you can get the seller to cover, either by the seller doing them or the seller giving you the money when you close the escrow? Is the seller willing to pay for any of the closing costs? If you're in a buyer's market, you may find the seller will bargain with you to get the house sold.

Not listening to the home inspector. After your offer is accepted, you'll pay for a home inspection to examine the property's condition inside and out. Understand that the results will only tell you so much.

Not all inspections test for things like radon, mold or pests, so be sure you know what's included. Also be sure the inspector can access every part of the home, such as the roof and any crawl spaces.

Attend the inspection and pay close attention. Don't be afraid to ask your inspector to take a look at something. Ask questions, no matter how silly they may be.

Never ask, "Should I buy this house?" No inspector will answer that one! You get to make that decision after reviewing the report and seeing what the seller is willing to fix. If you don't like it, you can always walk away and look at another house.

Action Items

- If you are serious about buying a house, calculate the maximum mortgage you will be able to afford, keeping in mind that is the *maximum* you feel comfortable paying.
- Interview at least three real estate agents to find one who you get along with. As with any profession, some are more experienced, while others are more aggressive; find an agent who shares your vision and personality.
- Get preapproved for a mortgage. It will help in the negotiation process.
- Try to control your emotions. This is probably the biggest purchase you will ever make, so if it does not feel "right", it is OK to walk away.

CHAPTER 12

INVESTING

The four most dangerous words in investing are "this time it's different."

—Sir John Templeton

It's not whether you're right or wrong that's important, but how much money you make when you're right and how much you lose when you're wrong.

—George Soros

If you have trouble imagining a 20% loss in the stock market, you shouldn't be in stocks.

—John Bogle

Investing can seem like a risky, complex process. With endless combinations of investment vehicles to choose from, just thinking how to invest can be difficult, especially knowing that all investments risk losing some or all of your money. So why bother?

Investing can help preserve your wealth by overcoming the effects of inflation, help you save for long-term goals (such as retirement or your children's education), and generate income so you can take a nice vacation. How can you get past all the negatives associated with investing? A helpful first step is to realize that you have time on your side.

Make a Plan

The key to financial security is to have a financial plan. You'll first need to figure out where you're starting from—for example, how much you owe and how much money you have saved. Then set your goals. Do you want a car, a college education for your children, or a comfortable retirement? Once you know what you want, when you want it, and how much it costs, you can figure out how much you'll need to save.

Save and Invest for the Long Term

Perhaps the best protection against risk is time. On any given day the stock market can go up or down. Sometimes a market downturn can last for months or years. Investors who adopt a buy-and-hold approach tend to come out ahead of those who try to time the ups and downs of the market.

Time is one of the most important factors determining how much your money will grow. If you saved $5 a week at 8% interest starting from the time you were eighteen years old, by age sixty-five your savings would total $134,000. If you wait until you are forty years old to begin saving, you'll have to save $32 a week to have $134,000 at age sixty-five. In fact, just one year's delay—waiting until you're nineteen instead of eighteen to start saving $5 a week at 8% interest—would cost you more than $10,000 by the time you're sixty-five.

Stocks and Bonds

Stocks and bonds are the two main vehicles that you are likely to invest in.

Stocks are when you have an ownership stake in a company. Many stocks pay dividends, which are a distribution of profits to the owner. Stock prices will change based on many factors, such as the economy, the company, market conditions and even how much they pay in dividends.

Bonds are loans made to an organization or government. When you invest in a bond, you generally receive periodic (monthly, quarterly or annual) interest payments. The value of a bond may go up or down depending on the economy, the company you are lending to and the interest rate the bond is paying.

Stocks are generally considered riskier and more volatile than bonds. However, there are many different kinds of stocks and bonds, with varying levels of stability, risk and return.

Mutual Funds

A *mutual fund* is a collection of stocks and/or bonds. Your money is pooled with the money of other investors into a fund that is invested in anywhere from a few dozen to hundreds of different stocks, bonds or both. The fund is managed by an expert who takes a fee and reports to a board of directors, providing you with relatively inexpensive professional money management.

Mutual funds make it easy for you to own a small portion of many investments. A "total stock market index fund", for example, may own stock in thousands of companies.

Other Investments

Many people think of investing as just stocks and bonds. Keep in mind that owning real estate (your own house or rentals) is also a form of investing. You can also invest in a business, or purchase an insurance policy (known as an annuity), or even have jewelry and gold. Each of these other investments has its own set of risks and rewards that should be carefully contemplated prior to investing.

Asset Allocation

Asset allocation means dividing your investments among different types of investments, such as stocks, bonds, and cash. The asset allocation decision is a personal one. An allocation that works best for you may change at different times in your life, depending on how long you have to invest, your cash needs and your ability to tolerate risk.

Factors to consider when thinking about your asset allocation include:

- *Time Horizon.* The number of months, years, or decades you need to invest to achieve your financial goal. If you have a longer time horizon, you may feel comfortable taking on riskier or more volatile investments. If you have a shorter time horizon, you may prefer to take on less risk.
- *Risk tolerance* is your ability and willingness to lose some or all of your investment in exchange for potentially greater returns.
- *Diversification* is when you allocate money among different investments to reduce risk. Don't put all of your eggs in one basket; if that basket crashes, there goes everything.

One way to diversify is to allocate your investments among different kinds of assets. Historically, stocks, bonds, and cash have not moved up and down at the same time. Factors that may cause one type of investment to perform poorly may improve returns for another type of investment. People invest in various types of assets in the hope that if one is losing money, the others make up for those losses.

You'll also be better diversified if you spread your investments within each asset class. That means holding a number of different stocks or bonds and investing in different industry sectors, such as consumer goods, health care, and technology. Once again, if one sector is doing poorly, you may offset it with other holdings in sectors that are doing well.

Ways to Invest

Online trading is quick and easy. With the click of a mouse, you can buy and sell stocks from one of the many online brokers offering low-cost trades. Although online trading saves investors time and money, it does not take the homework out of making investment decisions. You may be able to make a fast trade but not necessarily make wise investment decisions. Before you trade, know why you are buying or selling, the risk of what you are purchasing and your time frame.

You can get investment advice from many financial institutions, including banks, mutual fund companies and insurance companies. You can also hire, for a fee, a broker, an investment advisor, an accountant, or a financial planner to help you with your investment decisions. No matter what route you take, remember that it is your money, not theirs, so if you do not feel comfortable or do not understand their advice, you do not have to follow their recommendations.

Brokers execute trades for customers and are generally paid commissions when you buy or sell securities through them. Brokers may make recommendations about specific investments such as stocks, bonds, or mutual funds.

Brokerage firms vary widely in the quantity and quality of services they provide. Some have large research staffs and national operations; they can handle just about any kind of financial transaction you may need. Others are small and may specialize in promoting investments in unproven and risky companies. And there's everything else in between.

A *discount brokerage* charges lower fees and commissions for its services than what you'd pay at a full-service brokerage. But generally, you have to research and choose investments by yourself.

A *full-service brokerage* costs more, but the higher fees and commissions pay for a broker's investment advice based on that firm's research.

There is no such thing as a free lunch. Investment advisors and brokers do not perform their services as an act of charity. Be sure to inquire about fees prior to making any investment.

If a broker or advisor has initials after his name, don't assume that individual is better qualified than another. These titles are not all the same and do not necessarily mean better service for you. Some initials mean that the advisor or broker can only sell certain products and not offer you a complete menu of choices.

No Guarantees

All investments, including stocks, bonds, mutual funds and real estate carry the risk of losing some or all of your money, even when made through a broker, financial advisor or financial institution. If you are not able to stomach losing money, you should be careful what you invest in.

Be sure to read your statement every month. Seeing, in writing, how you have done may not be fun to look at when the market is down, but it is your most important protection against unauthorized transactions. If you find something odd or unusual, object, in writing, within ten days of receiving notification or you might not be able to contest it later.

Action Items

- Think about how much money you have to invest and what your future goals are.
- Learn all you can about stocks, bonds and other investments.
- Decide what way to invest is best for you and open an investment account.
- Fund the account as often as you can, watch how it is doing and make changes that you feel are appropriate.
- Be careful when receiving unsolicited advice.

13 CHAPTER

RETIREMENT

The best time to start thinking about your retirement is before the boss does.

—Unknown

Retire from work, but not from life.

—M.K. Soni

Retirement is like a long vacation in Las Vegas. The goal is to enjoy it the fullest, but not so fully that you run out of money.

—Jonathan Clements

One way humans stand out from other species is our ability to think and plan ahead. Unfortunately, since we are caught up in everyday life, most of us have trouble thinking about, and preparing for, the long term. It's difficult enough to plan something six months ahead, like a summer vacation, much less think about something far in the future, like retirement.

Estimating When You Can Retire

Government statistics show that, at age fifty, you've got about another thirty-four years to live; that's longer than most people's entire working career. With life expectancy increasing, you should probably think more like a forty-year retirement.

Retirement planning is a lot more than just picking an age to do so. It requires a realistic look at your lifestyle, your resources, your hobbies and interests, plus many other factors we tend to take for granted while working. Most of these elements, but not all of them, deal with money issues.

Determining What to Do in Retirement

Are you thinking of downsizing and relocating in retirement? Or maybe you'd love to start your own small business or consulting practice? Is your dream to stay in your family home and pursue hobbies and travel places you never got around to seeing? Determining what "retirement" means to you can help you figure out what your financial needs will be.

Consider Your Health

Thinking about your current ailments or conditions can help you determine potential medical costs in retirement. For example, if you're not able to be as active as you once were, you may want to get involved in community or volunteer work rather than make plans for world travel. Focusing on preventive care now also has the potential to minimize health care costs later, which will allow you to enjoy retirement.

Estimating How Much Money You Will Need

There are many online retirement calculators to help you estimate how much income you can plan on in retirement and what your financial needs may be. To get a realistic idea of how much you'll require, be sure to factor in what you want to do, along with possible health care issues and other considerations. Two suggested calculators are https://www.nerdwallet.com/investing/retirement-calculator and https://retirementplans.vanguard.com/VGApp/pe/pubeducation/calculators/RetirementIncomeCalc.jsf.

Remember, these calculators are just rough estimates. While they give you an idea of where you stand, the future is uncertain, so use some common sense when looking at the results.

Retirement Plan Options

It is never too soon to get started when saving for retirement. In addition to maximizing your non-retirement savings, here are some of the most common plans for you to consider:

401(k) or 403(b). In this type of plan, you choose a percentage of your salary each paycheck. That amount is deposited to a retirement account in your name. An advantage of this plan is that the amount you set aside is not taxed immediately but rather when you take it out during your retirement. Some employers match your contributions; be sure to take advantage of this since the employer's match is like a free bonus.

Traditional IRA. Individual Retirement Accounts (IRAs) allow you to accumulate earnings on your contributions tax-free. If you are not covered by a workplace retirement plan, you can contribute up to a certain amount ($6,000 in 2019) and deduct that contribution on your income tax returns. If you or your spouse participate in an employer's plan and your income is below certain income limits, you may be able to deduct some of your contributions. Once you are over age 70½, you must take distributions from the plan and pay tax on what you withdraw.

Roth IRA. In this plan, your contributions aren't deductible, but there are no required distributions when you retire, plus any amount you withdraw after reaching age 59½ is not taxable. There are income limits that affect who can contribute to a Roth IRA and limits on how much you can contribute each year

Solo 401(k). If you have a business, you can make contributions to either a traditional or Roth Solo 401(k) in amounts that are significantly higher than those for other retirement vehicles.

SEP-IRA. Simplified Employee Pension (SEP) IRAs are for small businesses. These plans have high contribution limits.

SIMPLE IRA. These plans are for businesses with fewer than 100 employees that want to offer employees a retirement savings option. The business makes contributions to individual employee accounts.

Note that each of these types of accounts is just where you park your money; you will have to consider investment options to maximize your long-term returns. For information on investments, see Chapter 12: Investing.

Social Security

Social Security is a federal retirement fund that you pay into through your paycheck or by being self-employed. The program also provides payments to those on disability and benefits to the spouses and children of covered workers who have died.

The Social Security system is based on the amount of credits that you earn as you work. Simply put, if you have worked a total of at least ten years in jobs where Social Security payments were deducted from your paycheck, you are eligible to receive benefits. Some government employees are not included in the Social Security system. In that case, you probably will not qualify for Social Security benefits but will qualify for your workplace pension.

How much you will collect depends on how many credits you have earned, your lifetime salary and the age when you begin collecting. The average benefit in 2019 is expected to be about $1,422 per month.

When you start will have a significant impact on how much you receive each month, so timing is an important consideration. Here's how it works:

- You can begin taking benefits as early as age sixty-two.
- You will receive your full benefits if you begin taking Social Security at full retirement age, which, depending on the year you were born, is between ages sixty-six and sixty-seven.
- Your benefits will be permanently reduced if you start taking them between age sixty-two and the full retirement age, somewhere between ages sixty-six and sixty-seven. That reduction ranges from 25% to 30% of what you would have received if you waited until full retirement age to begin.
- If you wait and begin taking payments at age seventy, your payments will increase by 8% for every year you wait. In any event, there is no reason to wait past age seventy to begin collecting your benefit.

How do you decide when to begin? Some factors to consider include your:

- current cash needs (do you need the money or can you wait?);
- other expected retirement income (can you take from other places instead of Social Security?);
- health and family longevity (the longer you live, the later you can begin taking Social Security); and
- post-retirement plans (do you need the money to do what you want to do?).

Action Items

- Start saving for retirement as soon as possible (like now!). If your employer has a plan, sign up for it and put aside as much as possible. If you are not covered by a plan, set up an IRA and fund it every year.
- Think about when you might want to retire and what you would do when that happens.
- Be sure your earnings are properly reported to Social Security and get a rough idea of how much the benefits may be. You can find this by going to https://www.ssa.gov/site/signin/en/.

14 CHAPTER

WILLS AND LIVING TRUSTS

Always go to other people's funerals, otherwise they won't come to yours.

—Yogi Berra

Death is not the end. There remains the litigation over the estate.

—Ambrose Bierce

A son can bear the loss of his father, but the loss of his inheritance may drive him to despair.

—Niccolò Machiavelli

It's a fact: every one of us will die someday, we just don't know when.

What happens to your "stuff" when you are no longer around? How will you tell your spouse, children or others what you want done with your assets? Should you have a will or a living trust?

It is estimated that only about 20% of Americans have living trusts; should you join that 20%?

A Living Trust Is Different from a Will

A *living trust* (sometimes called a *revocable trust*) is a written legal document. When you create the trust, you place your assets, which you can still use during your lifetime, into this trust. When you die, these assets are transferred to the people you name in your trust (the *beneficiaries*) by your chosen representative, called the *successor trustee*.

A *will* is also a written legal document with a plan to distribute your assets upon your death. The *executor*, who you name in your will, oversees this process. Unlike a living trust, which is in effect while you are alive, a will does not begin until after you die.

Advantages of a Living Trust

A Living Trust Avoids Probate. With a valid will, your estate may go through *probate*, a court proceeding where your assets are distributed by an executor according to your wishes. A living trust, on the other hand, does not go through probate. This usually means a faster distribution of assets to your heirs—from months or years with a will down to days or weeks with a living trust. The successor trustee pays your debts and distributes your assets according to the instructions in the living trust.

A Living Trust May Save You Money. Since it is a more complex legal document, preparing a living trust will probably cost more than a will. In addition, after you get the trust prepared, you must also transfer your assets (bank accounts, stocks, real estate and even your automobiles) to the trust through separate paperwork; simply signing a living trust does not actually fund the trust.

In addition to the trust, you also create a *pour-over will.* This provides for the distribution of any assets you may have forgotten to include in your trust. If the total amount of assets you may have forgotten to include in your trust is more than a certain amount (currently $150,000 in California), the pour-over will, just like any other will, must go through probate.

While a will costs less to prepare, a living trust can save your estate money at the time of your death. Court costs for probating your will are taken from your estate and can exceed the cost of preparing the trust document, although for a simple, uncontested will, costs are often nominal. Unless you provide otherwise, there are typically no fees paid to your successor trustee.

When it comes to saving income or estate taxes, there is no substantial difference between living trusts and wills. For married couples with substantial assets, a living trust may provide some estate tax savings.

For people with small estates and young married couples with no children, a living trust is probably not necessary. But as your life changes and you mature, it should be considered.

A Living Trust Provides Privacy. One big difference between the two legal documents is the level of privacy offered with a living trust. Since a living trust is not made public, upon your death your estate will be distributed privately. A will, on the other hand, is public record, so the whole world can know your affairs.

Another difference is the handling of out-of-state property you own upon your death. With a will, property must go through probate in their corresponding state; a living trust can help you avoid those probate hearings and costs.

Other Thoughts

A living trust is written in a way that your successor trustee can take care of your affairs if you become ill or incapacitated. Also, your handpicked successor trustee can manage your affairs without court intervention. If you simply have a will and are unable to take care of yourself, the court will appoint someone (a *guardian* or *conservator*) to oversee your affairs. That person will have to report to the court for approval of expenses, sales of property, and so on.

No matter what you choose, a will, living trust or neither, you should have a *durable power of attorney.* This document, one for financial and another for health care decisions, can avoid a court-appointed conservator for your affairs.

Note that both a living trust and a will allow you to choose a guardian for your children in the event of your death. Also, both can be changed and amended if your life situation changes.

Creating a Will or Living Trust

Everybody, not just rich people, should, at a minimum, have a will. You don't need to hire somebody to do it for you; in California you can easily fill in the blanks with the form at https://www.calbar.ca.gov/Portals/0/documents/publications/Will-Form.pdf.

If you want to name somebody in case you are too sick to take care of yourself, a free form can be found at https://oag.ca.gov/sites/.../ProbateCodeAdvancedHealthCareDirectiveForm-fillable.pdf.

To name somebody to take care of your financial affairs, a form can be found at https://www.allsaintsbh.org/wp-content/uploads/CA-Power-of-Attorney.pdf.

If you decide on a living trust, creating the trust agreement depends on your level of comfort in preparing documents. You can use, in increasing order of cost, one of many web-based services, a paralegal, or an attorney.

Action Steps

- Check to see if you have a will or a living trust already in place. If you do have a living trust, be sure that all of your assets have been placed in the trust.
- If you are single and don't have many assets, prepare a will, an advanced care directive, and a power of attorney. Make a copy and give it to your executor.
- If you are married, have children, or have assets over $150,000, consider preparing a living trust. Be sure to transfer your assets to the trust after it is prepared!
- Whatever you decide, don't put it off. The time to plan is now, not when it is too late.

15 CHAPTER

GIVING BACK

We make a living by what we get. We make a life by what we give.

—Winston Churchill

It is every man's obligation to put back into the world at least the equivalent of what he takes out of it.

—Albert Einstein

When you're in a position to have gotten so much, the gift at this point is giving back.

—Paul Stanley

Many wealthy Americans give to charity because they get a tax deduction for it. While this is certainly one motive to give, financial literacy is not just about making money; it includes giving back to the community.

Investigating a Charity

Prior to giving to any charity, you should examine their financial health. Most non-religious charities (but not government organizations) file an annual tax return with the IRS (Form 990). Start investigating a charity you are considering giving to by going to https://www.guidestar.org/Home.aspx and downloading their latest Form 990.

If you don't see the charity listed, the charity may be small, religious or governmental, so they don't have to file the return, or perhaps go under another corporate name. On the other hand, they may not be a legitimate charity. While not having a recent Form 990 is not necessarily a "red flag", in times of crisis (like a hurricane or other natural disaster), fake charities do pop up, so be particularly wary in those cases.

What to Look For

Some individuals like to give to small charities, while others like large, nationally known organizations. You can decide for yourself once you find the Form 990 by investigating these items:

- *Program Expenses.* Most well-run organizations spend at least 75% of expenses directly on their programs. That means that most organizations should spend no more than 25% of their total costs on administration and fundraising. To determine the percentage going to programs, go to page 10 of a charity's Form 990 (Statement of Functional Expenses) and find line 25 (total functional expenses). Divide column B (program services) by column A (total expenses), then multiply by 100. That is the percentage that organization is spending directly on their programs and services.
- *Types of Support.* Go to page 9 of Form 990 (Statement of Revenue) to discover a charity's funding sources. Some charities rely heavily on membership dues (line 1b) or government support (line 1e), while others survive almost solely on individual contributions (lines 1c and 1f), and still others depend on running programs (line 2g). Having multiple sources of revenue can be

beneficial for a charity. Also see how much of their revenue comes from their investments (line 3) or fundraising events (line 8).

- *Executive Pay*: On page 7 of Form 990 (Compensation of Officers, Directors, etc.), you can find the CEO's pay and any current officers and employees making over $100,000 annually.
- *Financial Stability*: On page 11 of Form 990, you learn what the organization owns and to whom they owe money.

Finally, check out their website. For example, do they list their charity's staff and board of directors? How do they make their financial information available? Plus, see if the charity is really doing what they say on the Form 990 you just reviewed.

Tax Benefits

A gift to a qualified charitable organization may qualify for an income tax deduction, but you must itemize your deductions in order to take that charitable deduction (see Chapter 7: Income Taxes for a discussion of how taxes work). There are limits to how much you can deduct, but they're very high.

When is it deductible? A contribution is deductible in the year in which it is paid (putting a check in the mail to the charity counts). A contribution made on a credit card is deductible in the year it is charged to your credit card, even if you pay the bill later.

What charities qualify? Many, but not all, charitable organizations qualify for a charitable contribution deduction. Contributions to individuals, foreign governments, foreign charities, and certain private foundations are generally not deductible. For charities that are not religious or governmental, you can see if they qualify for a deduction by going to https://apps.irs.gov/app/eos/.

What records do I need to keep? If you want to claim a charitable deduction for a cash donation, you must be prepared to verify the amount. In other words, you cannot deduct the spare change dropped in a charity's collection bucket without the proper documentation.

If you are audited, the IRS will accept one of the following to prove you gave money to a charity:

- a canceled check;
- a credit card statement;
- your bank statement showing the withdrawal and the name of the charity; or
- a written acknowledgment from the charity with the amount you gave.

If you contribute $250 or more, you must get a receipt from the charity that will include if you got anything back in return for your donation.

How about non-cash donations? You do not just have to give cash; non-cash donations can be allowed as a deduction.

If you contribute something that you have owned for more than one year, you can claim a deduction of how much the property is worth (the fair market value). Thus, it helps if you donate, rather than throw out, old clothes, furniture, and equipment that you no longer use.

The IRS only permits deductions for donations of clothing and household items that are in "good condition or better." Be sure to get a receipt, and if you donate a lot of stuff, take some pictures to prove the condition.

Be wary of donating a used vehicle since the donation is very limited.

Giving Time Instead of Money

It is hard to imagine where our community would be today if it wasn't for the help of volunteers that help others. Volunteers perform a variety of tasks for charities, such as stuffing envelopes, feeding animals, tutoring children, building houses, being a museum docent, counseling those in crisis, selling tickets, and answering phone calls.

Many volunteers serve on the board of directors and run the organization. If you are considering giving your time, here are steps to consider so you maximize the experience for both you and the charity you assist.

Identify charities that match your interests. Similar to donating money, begin your research by determining what it is you want to accomplish and identifying charities that work to achieve those goals. Look around your neighborhood to see what the needs are and if there are charities that accomplish them. An online search might also be helpful.

Think about what you can offer. Contact your list of potential charities to see if your skills match those needs. Think about things like how much time you can realistically give to them, what talents you have to help them, and what you personally hope to gain from the experience.

Since many charities have paid volunteer coordinators, don't be surprised if you are interviewed for the position. You may even be required to undergo a background check and training once you are accepted into their program.

Make a commitment. Once you identify a charity and are offered a volunteer position, it is important that you make a personal commitment to help the organization. Volunteers that show up late, cancel at the last minute and produce limited results are of limited use to most businesses, much less charities. A reliable volunteer with a strong work ethic can go a long way toward helping a charity meet its goals.

Remember: the organization has made an investment in you and is depending on you to fulfill your commitment.

Note that the donation of time is never a tax deduction. However, miles driven for and goods donated to the charity might be deductible.

Action Items

- Think about what needs there are in your community.
- Do a search to find a charity that helps fulfill that need.
- Obtain the charity's Form 990 and see if this is an organization you feel comfortable helping.
- Consider volunteering your time or making a donation to help that charity succeed in their mission.

ADDITIONAL RESOURCES

Books

Personal Finance for Dummies by Eric Tyson, 9th edition, 2019. Provides basic information in an easy-to-read format.

***Get a Financial Life: Personal Finance in Your Twenties and Thirties* by** Beth Kobliner, 2017. Practical tips for young adults.

***The Millionaire Next Door* by** Thomas Stanley & William Danko, Longstreet Press, 1977. Provides real-life examples of how you don't have to be flashy to be rich.

The New Frugality by Chris Farrell, Bloomsbury Press, 2010. Suggestions on how to lead a lifestyle without excessive spending.

Rich Dad, Poor Dad by Robert Kiyokaki, Plata Publishing, 2017. Alternative ways to think about money.

Online

Check credit history: https://www.annualcreditreport.com/index.action

Identity theft information: https://identitytheft.gov

Federal taxes: https://www.irs.gov/

California taxes: https://www.ftb.ca.gov/

Social security: https://www.ssa.gov/

Investing basics: https://www.360financialliteracy.org/Topics/Investor-Education/Investing-Basics

Retirement planning: https://www.fidelity.com/retirement-guidance/overview

Wills and living trusts: https://www.investopedia.com/articles/4personal-finance/051315/will-vs-trust-difference-between-two.asp

INDEX

ABOUT THE AUTHOR

In 1979, Howard J. Levine formed an accounting firm in the Los Angeles area. Until its sale in 2016, the office was well known for bookkeeping, accounting, tax return preparation, tax planning and consulting for small businesses, partnerships and corporations, as well as tax exempt (nonprofit) organizations and private foundations.

As a college professor and in private practice, plus experience with national accounting firms, Howard created a diverse client base and a wealth of experience, providing accounting and tax services to a unique group of clients nationwide. These clients ranged from small retail businesses, physicians, restaurants and a variety of service businesses, to nonprofit organizations and private foundations with budgets from under $100,000 to assets over $100 million.

Howard has served as both a member and Southern California coordinator of the Technical Review Panel of the California Board of Accountancy. He has written questions used on the CPA examination and has served on the board of numerous organizations as board member, treasurer and president. Howard served as a trustee of the California Society of CPAs Group Insurance Trust and as a member of the Internal Revenue Service Taxpayer Advocacy Panel.

Howard is currently a professor of accounting at Los Angeles Valley College. He is a CPA as well as a diplomat and life member of the American Board of Forensic Accountants.

OTHER BOOKS BY HOWARD J. LEVINE:

Accounting Ethics, A Practical Approach

The Greatest Book Ever Written, What the Bible Is Telling Us - Today

Made in United States
North Haven, CT
04 November 2026

21772136R00069